WHO LET THE DOG IN?

written by Deputy Becky Coyle

Illustrated by juanbjuan oliver

Dedicated to the Williamson County Sheriff's Department SRO Division, Williamson County Schools, and to Kinsley, Dallas, Thea, and Marley Rose.

Special thank you to Mrs. Maggi Margaret Turner, who made this book project possible.

-Becky

Designed by Flowerpot Press
in Franklin, TN.
www.FlowerpotPress.com
Designer: Stephanie Meyers
Editor: Katrine Crow
CHC-1010-0429
ISBN: 978-1-4867-0941-0
Made in China/Fabriqué en Chine

3 1461 00356 0227

Hi, my name is Becky. I am a deputy sheriff and school resource officer. I love teaching children just like you the importance of being safe while they are playing and learning at school.

Sometimes it is hard to understand why you have to practice drills and follow school rules, but being prepared is an important part of keeping your school safe. Your teachers, school officer, classmates, and even YOU play an important role in ensuring that your school is a place where you can do all of the things that you love to do! By working together and following the rules, we can accomplish so much!

For more information, discussion topics, and activities, visit my website!

www.Cops4Schools.com.

Stay safe,
Deputy Becky Coyle

Why are there officers that work in our schools?

Is it to arrest us for breaking the rules?

NO! It's to protect us and teach safety, too.

Now when someone wants in, we'll know what to do!

It's time for assembly! The kids all sat down.
In walked the guest speaker named Officer Brown.
She spoke about safety that works best in schools.
"The safety is simple—just follow the rules."

"Someone's visit to school should only begin

when they come in the front, and then they sign in.

Kids should not open doors to let guests inside.

Check with teachers or staff—let them be your guide!"

And then...

Later on in the day, it was time for snack,
so Ms. Blue left and said she would be right back.

Then, Marley heard a noise coming from outside.

"Did you hear that scratching?"

"I did," Sam replied.

"My little dog, Mookie, makes that noise as well.
He will scratch at the door—he can't ring the bell."

"A puppy?" said Sandra. "Outside in this storm?

We should let him come in so he can get warm!"

"But that's breaking the rules. I don't think we should.

Letting strangers inside will not turn out good!"

"IT sounds like a puppy. Don't worry at all!
I think IT is friendly, all furry and small!"
So then they all waited, then heard IT again.
Sandra ran to the door and she let IT in!

IT jumped in the room and ran by in a blur!

A big, scary monster with stinky, wet fur!

IT shivered and IT shook! IT showered them all!

IT jumped over three desks, then bounced down the hall!

Ms. Blue tried to catch IT, but that was quite hard.

It turned out that IT was a BIG St. Bernard!

Ms. Jones tried to grab him, but tripped and then...CRASH!

She fell and then her head got stuck in the trash!

"Who let the dog in? Where does he belong?

He's too hard to catch! He's so BIG and STRONG!"

From doorway to doorway and all through the halls,

he jumped, and he bounded, and bounced off the walls!

That's when someone yelled out, "Hey Kingston, sit down!"

The dog slammed to a halt and plopped to the ground.

In walked Officer Brown while shaking her head,

"I hope that this taught you a lesson," she said.

"Kids should not open doors to let guests inside.

Check with teachers or staff—let them be your guide!"

"Can anyone tell me why we have this rule?"

"We sure don't want strangers, or DOGS, in our school!"

"Never open the doors to let someone in!
A stranger, a parent, a DOG, or a friend!
School safety is simple—just follow the rules.
That's how you best help with protecting our schools!"

"We all know it makes sense to listen to you.
You say keep the door closed, and that's what we'll do!"

"See you tomorrow!"